Original title:
Frosty Silence

Author: Linda Leevike
ISBN HARDBACK: 978-9916-79-819-5
ISBN PAPERBACK: 978-9916-79-820-1
ISBN EBOOK: 978-9916-79-821-8

Muffled Footsteps in White

In the hush of falling snow,
Footsteps fade, a soft echo,
Nature whispers, secrets kept,
As the world in silence slept.

Pale moonlight bathes the land,
A canvas drawn by winter's hand,
Each step a story, softly spun,
Woven 'neath the quiet sun.

Chill bites at fingertips,
With every breath, the frosty sips,
The night adorned in icy lace,
Every move finds a sacred space.

Trees bend low, dressed in white,
Guardians of the serene night,
Muffled laughter haunts the air,
Echoes linger everywhere.

Through the veil of crystal skies,
Dreams take flight, as silence cries,
In this realm of winter's grace,
Muffled footsteps find their place.

Glacial Murmurs

Whispers of ice, so crystal clear,
Echo deep, for those who hear,
Gentle streams beneath the freeze,
Caught in time's enduring tease.

Mountains stand, their peaks in snow,
Guardians of the winds that blow,
Glacial murmurs softly play,
A symphony of night and day.

Calm surrounds the frozen lake,
Ripples dance, as if to wake,
Nature sighs in quiet tones,
Amidst the ice, where beauty moans.

Stars reflect in frosted glass,
A fleeting moment, gone so fast,
Every glimmer, a timeless spark,
Guiding souls through the dark.

Touch of winter, soft yet bold,
Stories of the past unfold,
In glacial murmur, find your song,
Where the heart and earth belong.

Shadows in Subzero

In the chill of frozen air,
Shadows linger, unaware,
Silent forms drift through the night,
Wrapped in dark's embracing light.

Footprints vanish, whispers fade,
In this realm where dreams are laid,
Subzero thoughts in twilight haze,
Lost within the winter's maze.

Flickering light from candles glow,
Casting shapes in the deep snow,
Figures dancing, lost in time,
In this icy world, they climb.

Echoes call from distant trees,
Carried softly on the breeze,
Shadows gather, yearn to play,
In the stillness, they drift away.

Yet in the cold, there's warmth to find,
Hearts entwined, both brave and blind,
In shadows cast by starlit skies,
Subzero dreams will always rise.

Nightfall's Frigid Caress

As daylight fades to earthy gray,
Nightfall comes to gently play,
Frigid touch upon the ground,
In silence lost, no greater sound.

Stars emerge, a silver gleam,
Painting skies like a gentle dream,
Whispers float in crisp night air,
Soft caress, beyond compare.

Frosty breath upon my face,
In this serene, enchanted space,
Winter's magic holds me tight,
Wrapped in peace, a tranquil night.

With every step, the world is still,
As shadows dance upon the hill,
Night unfolds its velvet hue,
Cradling all, both old and new.

In nightfall's embrace, I find my rest,
Amidst the chill, I feel so blessed,
Frigid caress, a quiet song,
In the heart of winter, I belong.

Stillness Wrapped in White

A blanket lies upon the ground,
Soft whispers echo, without a sound.
Each flake dances, pure and light,
Wrapped in stillness, all feels right.

The world seems paused, in gentle rest,
Nature's secrets, softly dressed.
In this moment, peace does reign,
A quiet heart, free from pain.

Branches bare, their limbs embrace,
A tranquil beauty, time won't erase.
Footsteps hush on snowy lanes,
In this quiet, the spirit gains.

Here I stand, each breath so slow,
Feeling warmth beneath the snow.
With every flake, a dream takes flight,
Lost in stillness, wrapped in white.

A Quiet Respite from the World

In a corner, shadows play,
Worries drift and fade away.
The candle flickers, warmth draws near,
In this moment, all is clear.

Soft melodies fill the air,
A gentle hush, a whispered prayer.
Clouds of thought begin to part,
Finding solace for the heart.

Outside, chaos may unfold,
But in here, calmness takes hold.
Each breath taken, a step to peace,
In this quiet, worries cease.

Surrounded by the calm embrace,
Time slows down, we find our place.
In the stillness, dreams unfurl,
A quiet respite from the world.

Shimmering Tranquility

Beneath the stars, the lake does gleam,
Ripples dance, like a silver dream.
Whispers of night, a soft caress,
In the shadows, we find our rest.

Reflections shimmer, deep and bright,
A canvas painted by soft light.
Stillness reigns, as hearts align,
In this moment, all is divine.

Crickets sing a lullaby,
Underneath the vast, black sky.
Every heartbeat finds its place,
In shimmering tranquility's grace.

The world fades out, in velvet night,
Wrapped in peace, held tight and right.
Nature whispers, secrets shared,
In this silence, love declared.

Silence in the Heart of Winter

Snowflakes fall, like whispered sighs,
Covering earth beneath grey skies.
The world outside, a frozen dream,
In the stillness, silence gleams.

Bare trees stand, their forms abstract,
In the frigid air, they attract.
Nature's breath, a delicate sound,
Silence wraps the frozen ground.

Footprints lead to paths unknown,
Each step taken, a feeling grown.
In winter's heart, the world awaits,
In frozen breaths, the stillness states.

Amidst the chill, warmth grows inside,
In solitude, we learn to bide.
Silence speaks in beautiful ways,
In the heart of winter, we find our days.

Murmurs of the White Landscape

Snowflakes dance, a silent song,
Whispers weave where shadows throng.
Nature's breath, serene and bright,
Blankets soft in purest white.

Footprints trace a winding way,
Children laugh, then laugh at play.
Branches bow with heavy grace,
In this stillness, find your place.

Echoes linger, wild and free,
Murmurs blend with the old oak tree.
Silent tales of days gone by,
Underneath the open sky.

Crystal streams beneath the snow,
Time stands still, an endless flow.
With each breath, the world ignites,
In the hush of winter nights.

Stillness Among the Pines

Tall and noble, standing proud,
Whispered secrets in the shroud.
Pine trees sway, a gentle tune,
Underneath the silver moon.

Sunlight filters through the green,
Silken shadows, soft and keen.
Nature's arms embrace the air,
In this stillness, moments share.

Mossy carpets, fragrant ground,
Every heartbeat, nature's sound.
Tiny creatures call and play,
In the pines, they find their way.

Breath of life in every sway,
Time drifts slowly, dreams betray.
Magic weaves through bark and leaf,
In the stillness, find belief.

The Subtle Art of Chilling Time

Time stands still, like dew on grass,
In simple moments, memories amass.
A cup of tea, a soft, warm chair,
Moments linger, free from care.

Gentle whispers, evening glow,
Clock hands slow, let worries go.
Pages turn in tranquil light,
Words of wisdom, pure delight.

With every sigh, let burdens fade,
In the quiet, dreams are made.
Breath by breath, the hours drift,
In this stillness, hearts can lift.

Nature's rhythm, soft and deep,
Time's embrace, a tranquil keep.
Life unwinds as shadows cast,
In the stillness, find the vast.

Beneath the Glimmering Frost

Beneath the frost, a world lies still,
Nature's hush, a tranquil thrill.
Crystals glisten, silver bright,
Whispers echo through the night.

Moonlight kisses every dome,
In this beauty, hearts find home.
Winter's breath, a soft caress,
Underneath the night's address.

Stars are twinkling overhead,
Softly guiding where we tread.
Every flake, a work of art,
Painting dreams on winter's heart.

In the silence, spirit calls,
Underneath the frosted halls.
Moments frozen, time stands still,
In this wonder, find your will.

Pas de Deux in the Snow

Two dancers glide through white,
Footprints lost in softly falling light.
Their laughter swirls like flurries,
In the stillness, time hurries.

As shadows mix with twilight's glow,
In a world untouched by sorrow's flow.
Each step an echo, a silent song,
Together, where the heart belongs.

Frozen breaths in the crisp night air,
Whispers shared without a care.
They spin as one, a gentle twirl,
In this snowy, dreamlike whirl.

Frosted branches arch above,
Nature's stage, a scene of love.
In the moonlight, they intertwine,
Creating paths, their souls align.

As dawn approaches, shadows fade,
Yet memories linger, never strayed.
In the quiet of the frost-kissed morn,
Two hearts dance, perfectly reborn.

Veiled in Whispered Frost

Mornings draped in silver sheen,
Underneath, a world unseen.
Whispers float on icy breath,
Nature holds its quiet death.

Trees adorned with crystals bright,
Glisten softly in the light.
Each flake tells a story old,
Of warmth beneath the frost's hold.

Footfalls crunch on frosted ground,
Echoes linger all around.
In silence, secrets softly shared,
Winter's hush, a love declared.

Veils of snow that gently fall,
Transforming landscapes, nature's thrall.
A canvas pure, untouched by hand,
In this stillness, hearts may stand.

The sun will rise, the frost will fade,
But memories of this hour made.
In every flake, a tale preserved,
Whispered dreams, forever served.

Shadows of a Snowy Twilight

Twilight spills its muted hue,
Across the ground, a blanket new.
Shadows stretch and softly play,
In the fading light of day.

Echoes linger in the chill,
As the world grows calm and still.
Footprints lead to paths unknown,
Winter's embrace, a heavy throne.

Branches weave a lace-like frame,
As darkness falls, it calls your name.
Each breath hangs in a frosty glass,
In the twilight, moments pass.

Beneath the stars, a silent dance,
In every swirl, a fleeting chance.
The night whispers secrets low,
In shadows deep, a soft tableau.

As the moonlight bathes the land,
Winter's magic, pure and grand.
In snowy twilight, dreams ignite,
Transforming shadows into light.

Shimmering Stillness

In the hush of twilight's glow,
Stars begin to softly show.
Night wraps all in velvet grace,
Silence finds a sacred place.

Moonlight dances on the stream,
Whispers weave like fragile dreams.
Stillness reigns, a cherished space,
Time suspended, nature's face.

Every leaf, a story told,
In the dark, the world feels bold.
Shadows play, and hearts align,
In this moment, we're divine.

Crickets sing their lullaby,
As the stars begin to sigh.
Wrapped in stillness, we unite,
In the shimmer of the night.

Breathe it in, the calm and clear,
Find the peace that lingers near.
In the quiet, love resides,
In this shimmering, still tide.

Secrets Beneath the Ice

In winter's grasp, a world concealed,
Mysteries of ages, revealed.
Beneath the frost, life waits and weaves,
Nature whispers, softly breathes.

Icicles hang like frozen tears,
Guardians of forgotten years.
Underneath the blanket white,
Hidden tales from day and night.

Cracks in ice, a story speaks,
Of secret paths and gentle creeks.
Silenced echoes in the cold,
Silent wonders to behold.

Life awaits the warmth of spring,
Underneath, a vibrant thing.
Yet for now, in peace, it lies,
Wrapped in dreams beneath the skies.

Close your eyes and feel the pull,
Of secrets deep and beautiful.
Nature's heart beats slow and wise,
In the silence, truth complies.

The Quietude of Winter's Breath

A breath of chill sweeps through the trees,
Whispers dance upon the breeze.
Calm descends in layers deep,
Nature's song invites our sleep.

Frosty branches, pure and bright,
Caught in winter's gentle light.
Each flake a miracle in flight,
Cloaks the world, a wondrous sight.

In quietude, the heart finds peace,
As all the clamor starts to cease.
Silent moments, filled with grace,
In this stillness, we embrace.

Footprints echo on the snow,
Marking paths where we will go.
In the hush, a promise made,
Of joy to bloom and never fade.

Listen closely, hear the call,
Winter's breath enfolds us all.
In the quietude, we grow,
In the heart of winter's glow.

Veils of White and Whispered Dreams

Veils of white on mountains high,
Kissing clouds that softly sigh.
In each flake, a dream descends,
Whispered hopes where quiet bends.

Dreams take flight on winter's breath,
Embracing life, defying death.
In the stillness, hearts entwine,
Underneath the starry shine.

Fields of snow, a silent stage,
Playing out a timeless page.
Every shadow tells a tale,
Of whispered winds that softly sail.

Crystals sparkle, capturing light,
In the dusk, a world ignites.
Veils of white, a tender view,
Painting dreams in shades of blue.

As the night begins to fall,
Winter weaves her magic call.
In the veils where dreams take flight,
We find solace in the night.

Encased in Serenity

In a quiet nook, I breathe,
Where shadows dance like leaves.
The world feels slow, at peace,
In soft whispers, time weaves.

A gentle breeze, a sighing tree,
Nature's hush fills the air.
Colors blend in harmony,
Echoes linger, light and fair.

Beneath the stars, a guiding hand,
The moon casts silver beams.
Wrapped in warmth of twilight's band,
Dreams float softly, like streams.

Silent moments shared anew,
Hearts beat slow, in tune.
In this realm of tranquil view,
Life's a sweet, quiet tune.

Encased within this sacred space,
I feel my spirit rise.
In serenity's warm embrace,
I find my paradise.

Whispers of the Winter Moon

The winter moon, a silver sphere,
Glows softly on the snow.
Its light, a hush, draws near,
In the night, it starts to grow.

Every flake, a diamond bright,
Dances with the chill.
In the silence of the night,
Time seems to stand still.

Trees wear cloaks of white and gray,
Branches bowed with grace.
In its glow, dreams drift away,
Lost in a gentle embrace.

The world hushed, a solemn hymn,
Echoes through the air.
Life feels fragile, soft and slim,
Beneath the moon's bright glare.

With each beat, a whisper calls,
Secrets wrapped in light.
As winter's night softly falls,
All is calm, pure delight.

The Beauty of the Unspoken

In silence, beauty finds its way,
Where words are not enough.
A glance, a touch, a soft ballet,
Love's language can be tough.

The heart speaks loud in quiet gleams,
Whispers that softly sway.
In the stillness, hope redeems,
Silent truths lead the way.

Unseen bonds connect us deep,
With each breath, we share.
In the shadows, secrets keep,
A truth beyond compare.

In the spaces, meaning lies,
Glimmers in our gaze.
Beyond the noise, the quiet sighs,
A love that softly stays.

So let our hearts embrace the calm,
Find joy in all that's still.
In the silence, there's a balm,
A beauty time can't kill.

Chill in the Air

A chill whispers through the trees,
Crisp leaves crunch beneath our feet.
In the twilight, breezy tease,
Nature's cycle feels complete.

The air, a dance of life and cold,
Wraps around, a tender coat.
Stories of the brave retold,
In every breath, a warming note.

Clouds gather, a gray parade,
Skies wear a cloak of blue.
Under the billowy cascade,
Hope hides in every hue.

As dusk drapes the world in grace,
And shadows start to play,
In this moment, we embrace,
The chill that marks the day.

So let the winter's breath unfold,
In every heart, there's fire.
Through the chill, we feel so bold,
Craving warmth, we must aspire.

In the Embrace of Quiet Snow

Snowflakes fall with soft grace,
Blanketing the world like lace.
Whispers drift through frosty air,
Quiet moments, winter's prayer.

Footsteps crunch on frozen grounds,
Nature sleeps, all peace surrounds.
Moonlight dances on the white,
Wrapping dreams in still of night.

Branches bow with laden weight,
Time stands still, it's not too late.
In this hush, our souls can mend,
Embrace the quiet, let it blend.

With each flake that softly lands,
We are cradled in snow's hands.
A gentle sigh, the heart's soft glow,
In the embrace of quiet snow.

Spheres of Silence

In twilight's glow, the world retreats,
Whispers held in subtle beats.
Underneath a velvet sky,
Spheres of silence drift and fly.

Stars awaken with a blink,
In their light, we pause and think.
Time dissolves in starlit dance,
Wrapped in night's ethereal trance.

Crickets sing a lullaby,
Echoes soft where shadows lie.
In the stillness, thoughts take wing,
Silence speaks of everything.

Waves of peace in moonlit streams,
Carry gently all our dreams.
In this space where thoughts align,
Spheres of silence, so divine.

Translucent Echoes

A whisper floats on gentle breeze,
Carrying tales of ancient trees.
Every rustle tells a story,
Translucent echoes of past glory.

Sunlight filters through the leaves,
Dancing shadows, nature weaves.
Time's reflections gently sway,
In the calm of end of day.

Waves of sound, though soft and light,
Brush our hearts with pure delight.
In the stillness, we can hear,
Echoes linger, ever near.

Every moment, fleeting grace,
Lives in memory's warm embrace.
Translucent echoes softly call,
Inviting us to heed their thrall.

When the World Glistens

Morning breaks with golden light,
Dewdrops sparkle, pure and bright.
Nature wakes from dreamy night,
When the world glistens, hearts take flight.

Mountains stand in proud repose,
Kissed by sun, their beauty grows.
Fields adorned with diamonds fair,
Glisten joyfully everywhere.

Streams reflect the azure hue,
Carrying whispers, clear and true.
In this moment, time stands still,
When the world glistens, souls can fill.

Every heartbeat sings a tune,
In the light of sunny noon.
Nature's magic, pure delight,
When the world glistens, all is right.

Ghosts of the Bitter Wind

Whispers dance in the night air,
Floating on chill, silent breath.
Memories linger without care,
Haunting whispers of lost death.

Dark shadows weave through the trees,
Rustling leaves tell their despair.
Lamenting softly on the breeze,
Echoes of love lost in the air.

Frosty fingers touch my skin,
Chilling deep to the very bone.
I feel their pain, I feel their sin,
In this place, I am not alone.

Their stories swirl in the night,
Filling the void with ghostly lore.
As stars above flicker bright,
They call me closer to the shore.

Yet I stand firm in my fear,
Facing the ghosts with steady gaze.
The bitter wind, I choose to hear,
And walk among their haunting ways.

Labyrinth of Frosted Trees

In a maze of white and gray,
Branches twist and intertwine.
Frosted leaves layer the way,
A silent path, a twisted line.

Footsteps crunch in the still air,
Each step leads deeper within.
Nature's art, both rare and rare,
Where echoes of winter begin.

Shapes emerge in the glimmering haze,
Figures hidden, waiting still.
Lost in this frozen maze,
A chill runs deep; I feel the thrill.

Whispers call from the shadows near,
Guiding me further into the gloom.
Yet a thread of doubt draws near,
In this frosted, arboreal room.

With each turn, I feel the pull,
Of tales untold, of past life sings.
In this labyrinth, I am full,
Of dreams encased on icy wings.

A Quietude of Twinkling Stars

In the stillness of night's embrace,
Stars flicker like whispers of light.
A canvas dark, a cosmic space,
Where thoughts drift softly into night.

Each glimmer holds a silent tale,
Of galaxies far and unknown.
In their beauty, my worries pale,
In this vast universe, I'm shown.

Bathing in the starry glow,
I breathe in peace, I let it flow.
The quietude, a sacred theme,
Awakens long-lost childhood dreams.

Waves of stardust fall around,
A serene hush, a soothing balm.
In this moment, I am found,
In the cosmos, I feel the calm.

With each twinkle, hope is cast,
A promise held despite the dark.
In a quietude that shan't last,
The stars ignite my shining spark.

Gathering Clouds of Wonder

Clouds billow out, soft and grand,
Painting dreams across the sky.
A tapestry, touched by hand,
Where every shade dances high.

In their folds, secrets reside,
Stories spun with threads of gold.
A mystical world to confide,
With wonders waiting to be told.

Each puff a memory unfurled,
A sigh of joy, a drop of rain.
As they travel, thoughts are swirled,
Through quiet whispers, joy and pain.

Thunder rumbles, a soft embrace,
Nature's voice in a thunderous roar.
Within the clouds, I find my place,
As dreams and beauty gently soar.

Gathering clouds, the sky's delight,
In their shade, I linger long.
In this realm of transient light,
I am united, where I belong.

The Soft Touch of Icebound Air

In the hush of winter's breath,
Whispers echo through the trees,
Frost blankets the world in white,
A soft touch upon the freeze.

Moonlight dances on the ground,
Casting shadows, silver bright,
Every flake a story told,
In the stillness of the night.

Crisp and clear, the silence reigns,
Footsteps crunching on the snow,
Nature's peace, a gentle balm,
In the air, time seems to slow.

Winds that carry distant songs,
Through the branches, soft and fair,
Nature's lullaby unfolds,
In the soft touch of icebound air.

As stars twinkle overhead,
Dreams take flight on frosty wings,
In this realm of chill and calm,
Winter's heart in silence sings.

Tranquil Nights Under Frost

Underneath the silver glow,
Of a shrouded, winter's night,
Stars peek through the glistening hues,
While the world sleeps, bound by light.

Gentle whispers in the dark,
As the moon spills out her grace,
Every flake a fleeting wish,
In this vast and quiet space.

Trees adorned in icy lace,
Stand like watchmen of the night,
Guarding dreams that softly flow,
In the frost's embrace so tight.

In the garden, shadows play,
Where the silence weaves its spell,
Nature holds its breath in awe,
Tranquil nights, where secrets dwell.

With each breath, the cold ignites,
A warmth within the heart's core,
As we linger, hand in hand,
In winter's hush, forevermore.

Silent Crystals at Twilight

At twilight's bend, the world transforms,
Silent crystals in the breeze,
Glistening softly, nature's gems,
Whispering tales through frozen leaves.

The day fades into a dream,
Painting skies in hues of gold,
As shadows stretch and softly creep,
A tranquil lull, a story told.

Each crystal holds a fleeting light,
Caught between the dusk and dawn,
Moments frozen, pure delight,
In the beauty of the lawn.

As darkness falls, the stars awake,
Crystals shimmer, bright and clear,
In the stillness, hearts will ache,
For the magic held so near.

So let the silent crystals gleam,
Under twilight's watchful gaze,
In their glow, we find our theme,
A moment lost in winter's haze.

Snowbound Reverie

In a world all draped in white,
Dreams of warmth and firesides glow,
Each flake a wish that drifts and falls,
In a snowbound reverie, we flow.

Voices soft like whispers shared,
Echo through the frosty air,
Laughter dances on the breeze,
In the love that's ours to bear.

Footprints left where love has trod,
In the field of shimmering white,
Where we wandered, hearts entwined,
In the magic of the night.

As the stars begin to fade,
And the dawn peeks through the trees,
We will cherish every snow,
Embraced in winter's gentle freeze.

Snowbound dreams, a cherished gift,
In the silence, we will find,
Every moment wrapped in bliss,
A reverie forever twined.

The Quiet Glint of Icicles

Icicles hang from the eaves,
Glistening softly in the sun.
Each shard a silent whisper,
Of winter's breath, just begun.

The world wrapped in crystal lace,
A tranquil spell in the air.
Time slows down in this embrace,
As peace resides everywhere.

Hushed echoes of falling snow,
Blanket secrets unexplored.
In the glow of twilight's show,
Nature's canvas is restored.

Gentle shadows start to creep,
As day bids a soft farewell.
In this moment, still and deep,
The icicles cast their spell.

Beneath the weight of frosty boughs,
Life pauses for just a breath.
In the quiet, nature bows,
To the beauty found in death.

Allure of the Snowbound Hour

The world transforms, stark and white,
Every step a crunching sound.
A gentle hush, the fall of night,
In this snowbound peace, I'm found.

Stars awaken in the clear sky,
While the moon casts silver light.
Embers of warmth from fires nearby,
Invite the heart to take flight.

Frosted branches sway and dance,
Underneath the velvet sky.
In the stillness, take a chance,
To breathe the air and just sigh.

Magic twinkles in each flake,
A wonder held in the cold.
Every moment, memories make,
As stories of winter unfold.

In the glow of winter's charm,
Time pauses, it's truly ours.
Wrapped in nature's softest calm,
We wander 'neath the snowbound stars.

Midnight's Icy Reflection

Under the shroud of midnight blue,
The world lies still, almost asleep.
In the darkness, dreams come true,
While shadows play, secrets to keep.

Frosted panes catch moonlight's grace,
A shimmering quilt spread wide.
In this tranquil, timeless place,
I find my heart, my mind, my guide.

Each breath forms a ghostly mist,
Whispers of chill on my skin.
In night's embrace, I can't resist,
The pull of the quiet within.

Thoughts dance like flames in the dark,
Flickering—silent and light.
In stillness, I find my spark,
As stars blink down from their height.

Time drifts like snowflakes in air,
Caught in the weave of the night.
In icy reflections, I dare,
To wander deep and take flight.

An Elegy Beneath White Breezes

Beneath the trees, a soft sigh flows,
As whispers weave through frozen air.
The ground, a soft and peaceful close,
Holds the memories now rare.

In the quiet, stories sleep,
Of summer days, long since gone.
The beauty wakes, faint but deep,
As winter's breath lingers on.

Each flake a tale, each gust a tune,
An elegy in white and grey.
While beneath this silver moon,
The past and present softly sway.

Lost moments dance on gusting winds,
A harmony of then and now.
Beneath the snow, life begins,
As dreams take root in hushed vow.

And here beneath these white breezes,
I linger, wrapped in nature's thought.
In winter's arms, my spirit eases,
With memories woven and sought.

A Canvas of Cold

The morning sky, a muted hue,
Blankets of snow stretch far and wide.
Whispers of winter, crisp and true,
Nature sleeps, in tranquil pride.

Trees don coats of frosted lace,
Branches bend beneath the weight.
Silence wraps this frozen space,
Time stands still, as if by fate.

Footsteps crunch on icy ground,
Echoes lost in stillness deep.
A fleeting moment, spellbound,
In the cold, the world does weep.

Shadows dance on the white expanse,
Every flake a work of art.
In this chill, there's magic's chance,
To find warmth within the heart.

As dusk falls softly, colors blend,
A canvas painted, stark yet bright.
Winter's touch, a lover's hand,
Cradles dreams in the quiet night.

Glistening Stillness

Underneath the sapphire sky,
Fields of white, untouched, so pure.
Every breath a misty sigh,
In this stillness, hearts endure.

Icicles hang like chandeliers,
Glistening in the soft, warm light.
A whisper carries through the years,
Tales of joy wrapped in the night.

Frosted petals, fragile grace,
Nature's art, a fleeting kiss.
In this moment, we embrace,
The gift of cold, the taste of bliss.

Stars above in crisp repose,
Watch the world in silent awe.
Winter's beauty gently glows,
A tranquil hush, a peaceful draw.

With each flake that graces ground,
Stories told of days gone by.
Here we stand, in peace, unbound,
Glistening stillness, love's soft sigh.

The Serene Veil of Frost

A gentle hush falls on the land,
The world is wrapped in a silver sheet.
Frost kisses softly, a lover's hand,
In this moment, time's heartbeat.

Windows glimmer with icy art,
Nature's canvas, a masterpiece.
Every detail plays a part,
In the quiet, we find peace.

Birds take flight on frozen wings,
Silhouettes against the pale.
Winter's tune, the quiet sings,
In every breath, a whispered tale.

Fields of white, where shadows blend,
Footprints mark a fleeting trace.
The frosty air, a gentle friend,
Wraps us close in its embrace.

As twilight falls, the stars ignite,
A serenade of silver glow.
The serene veil, a perfect sight,
Holds the world in soft, sweet flow.

Winter's Gentle Embrace

Softly now, the snow descends,
A blanket warm, yet chill remains.
In winter's hold, the silence bends,
Time whispers sweet, as daylight wanes.

Drifting clouds of cotton white,
Blanket all in gentle grace.
In the stillness of the night,
Hearts find solace, find their place.

Fires crackle, embers glow,
A cozy warmth within the storm.
Outside, winds begin to blow,
But here we nest, in safety's form.

As stars blink in the frosty skies,
Each twinkle tells a story known.
Winter's charm, in shivers lie,
Yet here in arms, we're not alone.

With every flake, a world anew,
In the soft embrace, we stay.
Winter's kiss, a sweet adieu,
Holds us close, till break of day.

Echoes of a Frigid Dawn

The sun appears, a timid glow,
Chasing shadows, soft and slow.
Whispers of frost in the biting air,
Nature wakes with a silent stare.

Branches glisten with icy lace,
As dawn's breath caresses the space.
Birds stir gently, a lullaby sweet,
Marking the day with a fragile beat.

Footsteps crunch on the frozen ground,
Echoes of life in the stillness found.
Each moment hangs like a fleeting dream,
Captured in time, a shimmering beam.

The world, a canvas of silver and blue,
Painted in hues, a breathtaking view.
With every heartbeat, the day unfolds,
A tale of warmth in the winter cold.

When Silence Wears White

In the stillness, silence reigns,
A cloak of white, soft as the rains.
Footsteps muffled, time stands still,
Wrapped in quiet, the heart to fill.

Trees stand solemn, draped in snow,
Nature's hush, a gentle flow.
Each breath visible, a clouded mist,
In this solitude, a tender tryst.

The world, a canvas, pure and bright,
Where shadows dance in the pale light.
Frozen whispers drift on the breeze,
Carried forth through the towering trees.

Underfoot, a crunch, a slight dismay,
Yet beauty lingers, come what may.
In white attire, silence takes its throne,
Echoing softly, we are not alone.

The Frozen Breath of Night

Stars twinkle in the velvet sky,
The moon hangs low, a watchful eye.
Nights of winter breathe a chill,
Whispers of magic, quiet and still.

The world wrapped deep in twilight's embrace,
Frosted fields in a silver lace.
Each breath, a wisp, a fleeting sight,
The frozen breath of a quiet night.

Crystal air and shadowed trees,
Sway gently in the nighttime breeze.
Stars conspire in a dance so fine,
Painting the dark with their celestial shine.

In this realm, where dreams reside,
The heart beats softly, a steady guide.
Beneath the cloak of the night so bright,
We find our solace, our inner light.

Glacial Serenade

Melodies rise from the frozen lake,
Nature's hymn that the wild winds make.
With each note, the ice starts to sing,
A glacial serenade, whispering spring.

Echoes of beauty in each icy breath,
Life awakens in the dance of death.
The frost, a blanket, tender and soft,
Hides stories of warmth, beckoning oft.

Pines stand tall, their secrets untold,
Guardians of dreams in the night so cold.
Under the stars, they sway and bend,
As the serenade plays, it knows no end.

In this symphony of ice and air,
Where silence lingers, a tranquil prayer.
We find our rhythm, our hearts aligned,
In the frozen dance of what we might find.

A Frozen Symphony

Crystal notes dance in the air,
Whispers of winter everywhere.
Each flake a sound, unique and bright,
Nature's song, pure and white.

The trees don coats of glistening lace,
Echoes of silence, an icy embrace.
The river freezes, a mirror so clear,
Reflecting dreams that draw us near.

Wind carries tales of frosty nights,
Under the stars, magical sights.
A symphony played by the cold and the bold,
Melodies from the stories untold.

Beneath the moon's soft silver glow,
Layers of ice begin to flow.
In each breath, a world made anew,
A frozen symphony we pursue.

Lost in the allure of this chilly scene,
Where hearts beat softly, serene and keen.
Harmony wrapped in a frosty guise,
A dance of dreams under starry skies.

Etched in Frosty Quietude

Footprints scattered in fresh, soft snow,
A world transformed, everything aglow.
Silence reigns, a peaceful sight,
Etched in frost, pure delight.

Branches hold delicate, glassy strands,
Nature's art created by cold hands.
Glimmers of ice shine in the light,
A canvas vast, a tranquil white.

Winter whispers secrets in the air,
Each breath a cloud, a moment rare.
Stillness wraps the earth so tight,
In frosty quiet, hearts take flight.

Glistening shadows dance and play,
As daylight fades, turning to gray.
Embraced by night, dreams take hold,
Stories waiting, softly told.

Echoes linger where chill winds blow,
In frozen realms, we learn to grow.
With every flake that falls from high,
We find the magic in winter's sigh.

Glacial Tranquility

A landscape vast in icy breath,
Where time slows down, escaping death.
Mountains rise with a glimmering sheen,
Guardians of peace, serene and clean.

Glaciers glide with a regal grace,
Moving slowly through this frozen place.
Every crevice tells a story untold,
Of nature's wonders, both fierce and bold.

In the stillness, a heartbeat's thrill,
Eyes closed, whispers of winter's chill.
Moments captured in a crystal frame,
Glacial tranquility, ever the same.

Stars twinkle in an endless expanse,
Hidden dreams in the night, they dance.
Under the moon's watchful gaze so clear,
We find our solace, our path to steer.

Wrapped in the hush of a world at ease,
Frozen moments that bring us peace.
In this quiet realm, we witness the art,
Of glacial tranquility, soothing our heart.

Where Dreams Hold the Chill

In silent nights where the cold winds weave,
Dreams take flight, in the frost we believe.
Snowflakes gather like whispers in our mind,
Where hopes and wishes intertwine and bind.

Underneath stars, a blanket of frost,
Imagined worlds, where nothing is lost.
Each breath we take is a glimmering chill,
In the space between dreams, we feel the thrill.

Pine trees sway with the weight of snow,
Guardians watching as soft breezes blow.
In the shadows, stories yet to tell,
Where dreams hold the chill, we know them well.

Frosty branches cradle silent nights,
Holding close the echoes of winter's flights.
Wrapped in warmth, yet kissed by the cold,
Our hearts awaken as the night unfolds.

As dawn approaches, colors ignite,
Transforming the world in soft morning light.
In a dreamscape, where chill vibes remain,
We surrender our worries to the frozen terrain.

Whispers of the Winter Gaze

Silent skies of muted gray,
Snowflakes dance and gently sway.
Trees stand tall in frosted robes,
Nature whispers, softly probes.

Footsteps crunch on snow so pure,
Every breath a cloud demure.
Fires crackle with warm embrace,
While winter paints a tranquil space.

Stars above in velvet night,
Glimmer softly, pure delight.
Moonlight bathes the world below,
In a magical, tranquil glow.

Hearts unite in cozy cheer,
Sharing warmth when friends are near.
Whispers float on chilling air,
Winter's beauty, beyond compare.

Memories dance in frosty breath,
Life finds joy amidst the death.
In winter's grasp, we find our peace,
A time for rest, a sweet release.

Crystals in the Stillness

Morning breaks with light so clear,
Crystals glisten, winter's cheer.
Each branch draped in silken white,
Nature's treasures, pure delight.

Silence wraps the world in grace,
Every flake a soft embrace.
Footsteps trace a quiet path,
In the stillness, echoes laugh.

Sunlight dances on the ice,
A wintry world, cold but nice.
Reflected shades in fresh spun frost,
In this beauty, we are lost.

Beneath the calm, life stirs awake,
As rivers flow and branches shake.
The heartbeat of the season sings,
In the hush, a joy it brings.

Whispers ride on frosty air,
Messages of love and care.
Crystals shine, bright and bold,
In the stillness, stories told.

A Shroud of Icy Quiet

Rivers slowed beneath the frost,
In winter's shroud, all seems lost.
Yet in silence, life remains,
A quiet depth in icy chains.

The world rests beneath the chill,
Snowy blankets, soft and still.
Every breath a frosty sigh,
Underneath a steel-gray sky.

Hushed whispers of the barren trees,
Carry softly on the breeze.
Each moment stretched in frozen time,
Nature's rhythm, slow but prime.

Footprints trace a secret tale,
As winter winds begin to wail.
Through the quiet, dreams take flight,
Wrapped in blankets of the night.

A shroud of icy quiet lies,
Beneath the cold and muted skies.
Yet hope warms the heart within,
For spring's sweet touch will soon begin.

Muffled Echoes of the Cold

In the still of winter's breath,
Life pauses at the edge of death.
Muffled echoes drift around,
As silence blankets all the ground.

Snow falls softly like a kiss,
Covering the world in bliss.
Quietude fills the freezing air,
Whispers of the season's care.

Branches bow beneath the weight,
Nature's beauty, still sedate.
Each flake tells a story old,
Of memories in winters cold.

Voices linger, soft and clear,
In this hush, we draw near.
Muffled echoes of the past,
In the cold, we find our cast.

With every breath, we cherish more,
What lay dormant, will restore.
Muffled echoes in the night,
Guide our hearts with gentle light.

Frost-kissed Echoes

In the hush of dawn's light,
Frost paints the world so bright.
Trees don a crystal crown,
Echoes of winter's gown.

Footsteps crunch on icy ground,
Nature's silence, profound.
Whispers wander in the air,
Memories we freely share.

Moonlight drapes the frozen lakes,
Sparkling like a dream that wakes.
Each breath forms a fleeting mist,
In the echoes, we persist.

Beneath the frosty, serene night,
Stars shine like gems, so bright.
Each moment, a fleeting glimpse,
In these frost-kissed winter limps.

Time drifts slow, as snowflakes fall,
Waltzing gently, answering the call.
In the quietude we find,
Peace within heart and mind.

Silence on a Snowy Eve

Snow blankets the world in white,
Softly falling, pure delight.
Whispers of the night grow near,
Wrapped in peace, no cause for fear.

Stars twinkle in the frosty sky,
Silent wishes drift and fly.
Each flake carries dreams anew,
In the silence, hope shines through.

Footsteps fade into the past,
Memories carved, meant to last.
Underneath this snowy shroud,
Voices hushed, emotions loud.

Fires crackle, warmth surrounds,
Joyful laughter, cheerful sounds.
Yet in moments, stillness reigns,
In the snow, love remains.

As night wraps its gentle hold,
Stories whispered, softly told.
Silence reigns on this eve,
In winter's arms, we believe.

A Still Heart in Winter's Grasp

Winter's breath, so cool and clear,
Wraps the world in love sincere.
Trees stand tall with arms outstretched,
Holding dreams that life has fetched.

Frozen rivers, still and deep,
Cradle secrets, quiet sleep.
Thoughts drift like snowflakes down,
Silent whispers all around.

In the stillness, hearts unite,
Sharing warmth through the cold night.
Every heartbeat, a soft glow,
In winter's grasp, love will flow.

The world shimmers like a dream,
In this quiet, life will seem.
Hope rises with the morning light,
A still heart, embracing the night.

Wandering through the winter's chill,
Finding peace and strength at will.
In the quiet, we discover,
The whispers of love, our true cover.

Whispering Winds in White

Winds whisper secrets of the night,
In the snow, the world feels right.
Gentle breezes softly sigh,
As winter's magic drifts by.

Branches sway with frozen grace,
Nature wears a soft embrace.
Every gust tells tales of old,
In the white, new dreams unfold.

Footsteps follow where they lead,
In the silence, hearts take heed.
Whispering winds, an ancient song,
In the cold, we all belong.

As moonbeams dance on snow-draped hills,
Every breath of winter thrills.
Echoes of the past we share,
Floating softly in the air.

Through the forest, winds will weave,
Stories held in frosty leaves.
In this magic, freely roam,
Whispering winds, our hearts find home.

Serenade of the Still Woods

In the hush of twilight's glow,
Whispers of the trees do flow.
Moonlight dances on the leaves,
Nature's song the heart receives.

Crickets chirp in soft refrain,
Echoing through the gentle rain.
A silver stream sings a tune,
Underneath the watchful moon.

Every shadow, every breeze,
Carrying tales through the trees.
The forest breathes, a sacred place,
Where time slows down, and dreams embrace.

A deer steps soft on mossy ground,
In this realm, calmness is found.
Stars peek through the leafy boughs,
Offering peace, in solemn vows.

In stillness, nature finds her voice,
In quiet harmony, we rejoice.
The woods hold magic, wild and free,
A serenade for you and me.

The Iced Artistry of Nature

Frosted branches glisten bright,
Underneath the pale moonlight.
Every flake a masterpiece,
Nature's art that brings us peace.

Icicles hang like crystal tears,
Reflecting all our fleeting years.
The world transformed in purest white,
A canvas drawn by winter's might.

Patterns swirl in icy breath,
Life embraced in gentle death.
Frozen rivers whisper low,
Secrets only they can know.

Brittle air, a chilling kiss,
In the silence, moments bliss.
Every step on powdered ground,
Echoes soft, a tranquil sound.

The artistry, both stark and bold,
Tales of winter yet untold.
In shimmering silence, calm and clear,
Nature's magic, ever near.

Snowfall's Embrace

Softly falling, flakes descend,
Covering the earth, a gentle friend.
Whispers secrets on the breeze,
Snowflakes twirl from frosted trees.

Each one unique, a delicate dance,
Caught in winter's spellbound trance.
Cocooned in white, the world transforms,
In snow's embrace, the spirit warms.

Children laugh, their joy displayed,
Building dreams in snowy glade.
Footprints lead to winter's song,
Where hearts unite and feel they belong.

As evening falls, the light grows dim,
Stars above in twilight's hymn.
Wrapped in blankets, warm and tight,
Love flows softly in the night.

Snowfall's embrace, a gentle grace,
Painting smiles on every face.
In this stillness, peace finds space,
A magical, serene place.

The Cloak of Deep Midwinter

Beneath the cloak of winter's chill,
The world is quiet, a breathless still.
Trees are draped in snow so white,
The stars burn on through the long night.

Crystalline silence fills the air,
Each heartbeat echoes a whispered prayer.
Bitter winds howl, fierce and cold,
Yet hidden warmth begins to unfold.

The hearth glows bright, inviting warmth,
As families gather, hearts to charm.
Stories shared by flickering light,
Creating memories, pure delight.

Outside, a realm of frozen lace,
Nature's hand has left her grace.
Underneath the starry dome,
In winter's heart, we find our home.

This cloak of deep, midwinter's night,
Wraps us in dreams, a soothing sight.
In its embrace, we linger long,
Finding comfort in winter's song.

Veil of White

In the morning's gentle light,
Snowflakes dance, a pure delight.
Blanket soft upon the ground,
Nature's hush, a tranquil sound.

Footsteps crunch, a whispering song,
Children laugh, it won't be long.
Snowmen rise with coal for eyes,
Winter's magic fills the skies.

Trees adorned in frosty lace,
A wonderland, a cozy space.
Crisp air carries joy and cheer,
Winter's touch is drawing near.

Lanterns glow, the world aglow,
Breath like clouds in evening's flow.
Underneath the moonlit sky,
Dreams unfold as snow drifts by.

Time slows down in winter's grasp,
Moments linger, memories clasp.
In the chill, warmth finds its way,
Veil of white, a bright display.

In the Heart of the Freeze

Icicles hang from branches bare,
Whispers drift in frosty air.
Silence deep, as shadows play,
In the heart where dreams delay.

Every breath a ghostly cloud,
Winter's grip is fierce and proud.
Underneath this frozen sea,
Life waits patiently to be.

Crystals shimmer on the ground,
In the stillness, peace is found.
Nature sleeps, the world is still,
In the heart, an iron will.

Time stands still, the sun seems shy,
With every twinkle, winter nigh.
In the quiet, hope resides,
Through the freeze, the spirit guides.

Moments linger, cold yet bright,
In the heart of the winter's night.
Awaiting spring, a gentle tease,
In the heart, amidst the freeze.

Stillness Beneath the Stars

Night unfolds, a velvet gown,
Stars like diamonds shining down.
In the quiet, whispers sigh,
Stillness reigns, the world goes by.

Mountains loom in shadowed grace,
Moonlight dances on each face.
Crickets sing a lullaby,
In the stillness, heartbeats sigh.

Time suspends in tranquil night,
Every twinkle feels so right.
Nature sleeps, and dreams take flight,
Stillness glows beneath the light.

Whispers of the night entwine,
Breath of calm, a world divine.
In this moment, peace will last,
Stillness holds the echoes past.

In the dark, the heart can see,
Beneath the stars, we're truly free.
A gentle hush, a sacred space,
Stillness found in time and place.

The Embrace of the Shiver

Chill winds weave through ancient trees,
A dance that hums with winter's freeze.
Each breath a cloud, the air so crisp,
In this moment, the heart will lisp.

Frosty fingers touch the night,
Embrace of shiver feels so right.
Nature's blanket, soft and white,
Cocooned in dreams till morning light.

Stars peer down, they seem to play,
Flickering lights in cold array.
Underneath the silver glow,
Embrace of shiver, soft and slow.

Firelight dances in the dark,
Warmth of hearts, a gentle spark.
In the chill, love finds a way,
Holding close, come what may.

So embrace the cold, don't shy away,
In the shiver, warmth will stay.
Life's a journey, winter's kiss,
In its hold, we find our bliss.

Soft Footfalls in the Cold

Snowflakes fall, a hushed delight,
Each footstep soft, the world is white.
Whispers echo in the air,
Winter's breath, a gentle prayer.

Trees stand tall, with arms outspread,
Casting shadows, where dreams are fed.
The moonlight glows on icy streams,
Night unfolds like tender dreams.

Footfalls linger, secrets shared,
Frosted paths, the heart is bared.
A quiet world, so still, so vast,
Each moment plays, a spell is cast.

Footprints lead where few have gone,
A fleeting dance, at break of dawn.
In the silence, feelings swell,
With every step, the stories tell.

Soft footfalls, a fleeting grace,
In winter's arms, we find our place.
Where echoes fade and hopes renew,
In the cold embrace, I walk with you.

The Gentle Hand of Winter

Winter breathes with gentle hand,
Fingers tracing on the land.
Glistening frost on every tree,
Nature wraps in purity.

A soft sigh from the frozen lake,
Underneath, the shadows wake.
Branches bow, as if to yield,
To the quiet, sacred field.

The sun peeks through a silver veil,
Casting light on winter's trail.
While cold winds whisper tales of old,
In their embrace, we are consoled.

Each flake that falls, a tiny gem,
Adorning earth, a diadem.
Hope is born with every chill,
A serene heart, forever still.

So let the winter's gentle grace
Fill each corner, every space.
In the stillness, life unfolds,
Held in winter's hands, like gold.

An Elegy in Ice

Silent echoes, a frozen sigh,
Memories drift as time slips by.
In the stillness, shadows blend,
An elegy, where dreams suspend.

Each crystal formed, a story told,
Of laughter lost and hearts grown cold.
Beneath the surface, whispers lay,
Frozen tears where hopes decay.

Time has painted all in white,
A ghostly dance in pale moonlight.
Ancient trees, like sentinels, stand,
Guarding secrets of this land.

Winds carry tales of those who roam,
In icy silence, far from home.
Yet beauty lingers, sharp and bright,
In this elegy, a fleeting light.

So let us mourn in tranquil peace,
For in each loss, a sweet release.
In the heart of winter's embrace,
An elegy finds its rightful place.

Reflections on a Bitter Stream

Bitter waters flow with grace,
Mirrored thoughts in liquid lace.
Shadows dart, elusive flight,
Chasing dreams into the night.

Frosted banks, edges untamed,
Whispers linger, feelings named.
Every ripple tells a tale,
Caught in silence, soft and frail.

Reflections dance on waters deep,
Secrets held, in silence keep.
Time meanders, never stays,
Flowing through the endless days.

Life's currents twist, turn, and bend,
All our thoughts, they twist and blend.
In the bitter, find the sweet,
Every journey bears its heat.

Yet here we pause, amidst the stream,
In the depths, we dare to dream.
Reflections linger, memories gleam,
In the heart of a bitter stream.

Breathless in the Blizzard

Whirling winds in a frosty dance,
Snowflakes kiss the earth's expanse.
Silent whispers fill the night,
Wrapped in cold, a pure delight.

Footprints vanish, a fleeting trace,
Nature's white, a soft embrace.
Breathless moments, hearts entwined,
In the storm, true peace we find.

Glistening flakes in twilight's hues,
Every flake, a story muse.
Beneath this shroud, the world's asleep,
In the blizzard, dreams we keep.

Branches bow, the trees stand tall,
Winter silence, a gentle call.
Time stands still in the frozen air,
Magic lingers everywhere.

Days may pass, but still we know,
In the heart, the blizzard's glow.
Breathless moments 'neath skies of gray,
In winter's arms, forever stay.

Subdued by Snowfall

Falling softly, a tender weight,
Snow blankets the world, a silent fate.
Each drift whispers secrets low,
In this tranquil, frosty glow.

Pine trees laden, dressed in white,
Held in quiet, pure delight.
Footsteps muffled, echoes fade,
Memories wrapped in the soft cascade.

Moonlight dances on a frozen stream,
In the night, we softly dream.
Every flake, a fleeting kiss,
In this snowfall, find our bliss.

Warmth inside as cold winds blow,
Holding close to love's sweet glow.
Subdued by snow, we find our way,
In winter's embrace, we choose to stay.

Seasons turn, yet still we keep,
In winter's heart, our secrets seep.
Subdued by snowfall, spirits rise,
In frozen moments, we find the skies.

April's Frosty Veil

A chilling breath in springtime's arm,
April wears a frosty charm.
Petals shiver, skies are gray,
Winter's touch will not delay.

Fields once green, now touched by ice,
Nature's dance, a fleeting slice.
Hope hangs in the chilly air,
With bated breath, we pause and stare.

Morning glistens, the world anew,
A fragile layer of glimmering dew.
Crisp and clear, each moment grows,
In April's hold, the beauty flows.

Yet warmth lingers, a hint of spring,
A promise wrapped in winter's wing.
Through every frost, the blossoms fight,
Breaking free to greet the light.

April's frost, a gentle veil,
Time will shift, the warmth prevail.
In every chill, a love we find,
As seasons change, our hearts rewind.

Echoes in the Winter Woods

Silent paths where shadows lie,
Whispers of the trees reply.
Footfalls soft on a snowy coat,
In the woods, wild dreams float.

Branches creak with tales untold,
Echoes ring in the bitter cold.
Moonlit trails weave through the night,
In the winter, hearts take flight.

The crunch of snow beneath our feet,
Each step a rhythm, bittersweet.
Nature's pulse in frosty air,
Echoes dance, a tranquil prayer.

Frozen lakes, a world asleep,
In the stillness, secrets keep.
Breathless beauty, shadows blend,
In winter's woods, our hearts transcend.

Voices blend with the howling breeze,
Carried forth among the trees.
Echoes linger, softly swirl,
In winter's hand, we gently twirl.

A Breath of Ice

Frost whispers on window panes,
Silent secrets of the night,
Each breath draws in the chill,
Glistening under pale moonlight.

Stars shiver in the dark sky,
As frost blankets the sleeping ground,
A world wrapped in silver sighs,
Where icy dreams are softly found.

Branches wear a crystal crown,
Nature's art in frozen state,
Amidst the chill, a gentle sound,
A breath of ice, we contemplate.

Footsteps crunching on the snow,
Echoes of a winter's hymn,
In this quiet, we all know,
Life waits patiently within.

Through the stillness, warmth will rise,
As seasons turn, the cold will fade,
Yet in our hearts the spirit lies,
A breath of ice, forever made.

Hushed Conversations of Winter

Winter wraps the earth in white,
Every whisper, soft and clear,
Branches speak of frostbite nights,
In the silence, we draw near.

Hushed conversations fill the air,
Snowflakes dance like fleeting thoughts,
Each flurry falls, a moment rare,
As time slows down, our worries caught.

The moon hangs low, a watchful eye,
Over quiet streets now bare,
Night reveals its velvet sky,
As dreams emerge, we breathe and share.

Footprints trace our subtle quests,
Silent stories on the ground,
In this season, we find rest,
Hushed, the world with peace surrounds.

Fires crackle, shadows play,
Warmth ignites the frosty chill,
In every heart, a wish to stay,
Hushed conversations, gentle still.

Crystalized Dreams

In the frigid breath of night,
Dreams rest softly on the ground,
Wrapped in frost, glimmering bright,
Crystalized, where hope is found.

Shadows linger, softly cast,
On the glistening fields of white,
Echoes of the day now passed,
In the stillness, hearts take flight.

Vision clear, like glass on fire,
Winter's breath, a whispered kiss,
Each moment, dreams reach higher,
In this cold, we find our bliss.

Stars like diamonds, brightly glow,
Guiding dreams through winter's chill,
In their light, we come to know,
Crystalized dreams hold time still.

With each dawn, a dance of light,
On the ice, our wishes gleam,
In the heart of winter's night,
Together, we pursue a dream.

The Sound of Cold

Listen close, the silence sings,
A symphony of winter's chill,
Frosted air with magic brings,
The sound of cold, a gentle thrill.

Crackling ice beneath our feet,
Nature's rhythm, crisp and clear,
Footsteps echo, soft and sweet,
The sound of cold is always near.

Windswept whispers through the trees,
Singing secrets as they sway,
A fleeting song upon the breeze,
The sound of cold will hold its sway.

Snowflakes flutter, soft ballet,
Falling lightly, one by one,
In their dance, they drift away,
Creating art beneath the sun.

As twilight wraps the world in night,
Listen for the quiet call,
In the calm, there's pure delight,
The sound of cold envelops all.

The Cold's Gentle Lullaby

The snowflakes dance in silent grace,
A whisper soft, a sweet embrace.
Under the moon's cool, silver glow,
Night wraps the world in a frosty flow.

Trees stand tall, their branches bare,
Crystals glisten in the chill of air.
Nature breathes in peaceful sighs,
As winter's song drifts from the skies.

Each breath of wind, a tender sigh,
The quiet warmth of dreams nearby.
Cradled in frost, the earth does rest,
Awaiting spring with hope, the best.

In this serene, enchanted space,
The cold's embrace, a soft embrace.
With every flake that meets the ground,
A lullaby of peace is found.

So close your eyes, and drift away,
Let winter's charm forever stay.
In dreams, we dance through nights so bright,
The cold's gentle hush, our guiding light.

Embracing the Chill

In the stillness, silence reigns,
Winter's aura, soft refrains.
Snow-laden paths, pure and white,
Embracing the chill, a pure delight.

The frosty air, so crisp and clear,
Brings forth laughter, joy, and cheer.
Against the cold, we come alive,
In snowy fields, our spirits thrive.

With scarves wrapped tight, and cheeks aglow,
We journey where the wild winds blow.
Each step we take, a crunching sound,
As winter's wonder wraps around.

The trees wear coats of shimmering ice,
A dazzling sight, so cold yet nice.
Hand in hand, we wander wide,
Embracing the chill, our hearts collide.

So let the frost weave tales untold,
In moments shared, we brave the cold.
Together we find warmth in despair,
In winter's arms, we're free to care.

The Icy Blanket of Night

Under the stars, a blanket lies,
Icy white, 'neath darkened skies.
Moonlight kisses each frozen seam,
The night unfolds a whispered dream.

Frosted crystals crown each hill,
A tranquil hush, the world stands still.
In the depth of cold, there's peace profound,
Nature's secrets softly found.

Beneath the dark, the shadows play,
With every breath, the night feels gay.
Wrapped in warmth, we hear the sound,
Of winter's heart, a gentle pound.

The world in slumber, lost in grace,
While starlight lays a tender trace.
The icy blanket covers all,
In its embrace, we feel the call.

So let us roam, where dreams take flight,
Under the spell of winter's night.
With every twinkle in the sky,
The icy blanket whispers by.

Shadows Beneath the Frost

In shadows deep, the frost does weave,
Stories told on winter's eve.
Silent footfalls on powdered ground,
Nature's secrets lost, yet found.

The trees stand guard, their branches bare,
As twilight whispers on the air.
Each breath of dusk, a chill takes hold,
While dreams of warmth begin to unfold.

Beneath the frost, the earth dreams tight,
Wrapped in whispers of gentle night.
As shadows lengthen and stretch out far,
The hope of spring shines like a star.

In the quiet, a promise stirs,
Of blooms to come, as winter blurs.
With every gust, the branches sway,
Shadows dance till break of day.

So linger here beneath the frost,
In winter's depth, we find what's lost.
The chill may bite, but hearts grow bold,
In shadows deep, our tales unfold.

The Palette of Winter's Breath

Whispers of white on the frozen ground,
Brushstrokes of grey where the shadows abound.
A canvas of stillness, the silence so deep,
Nature's reflection, in slumber's soft sleep.

Crimson and gold where the sunlight will play,
Hints of the warmth in the cold, crisp ballet.
Branches adorned with each glimmering flake,
Each moment a treasure, each breath a keepsake.

A frosty breath dances through branches so bare,
The song of the winter hangs sweet in the air.
In this artful season, the heart finds its peace,
In the palette of winter, all worries can cease.

The world takes on magic, a tranquil embrace,
Snowflakes unite in a perfect white lace.
While shadows grow longer, the dusk softly calls,
In the palette of winter, the soul gently falls.

So let us rejoice in this canvas divine,
In the beauty of winter, where dreams intertwine.
With each brush of frost on the world that we know,
The palette of winter reveals endless glow.

Dark Blue Shadows in the Snow

Night covers the land in a silken embrace,
Where shadows take form in this delicate space.
Dark blue whispers blend with the white,
Creating a dance of the day and the night.

Moonlight reflects on the soft, frozen sheet,
A symphony quiet, serene and discreet.
Shadows stretch long, in the stillness they flow,
In the heart of the winter, dark blue shadows grow.

Branches hang heavy, cloaked like a dream,
In the dark, there's a magic that glistens and gleams.
Every flicker of light, a gentle caress,
In the richness of night, the soul finds its rest.

Footprints mark paths in the innocent snow,
Tracing the stories of where we might go.
Dark blue shadows hold the secrets untold,
In their depths, countless memories unfold.

As stars twinkle softly in the cold, crisp air,
The world is a canvas, suspended with care.
In the mix of the dark and the bright evening glow,
We dance with the shadows and drift with the flow.

Hidden Among Frosted Pines

Where the frost weaves silver through evergreen trees,
A whispering breath floats with each gentle breeze.
Among the tall pines, secrets perfect and pure,
Nature's own magic, a place to endure.

Softly the snow blankets all in its grace,
Covering treasures in a luminous lace.
Frosted boughs glisten, a wonderful sight,
In the embrace of the woods, soft shadows ignite.

Step quietly forward, the world starts to gleam,
Hidden among pines, where all is a dream.
Every breath taken fills the soul with delight,
In the heart of the forest, lost in the night.

Muffled the echoes, the fears fade away,
In the hush of the woods, find peace where we stay.
Nature's enchantment cradles us tight,
Hidden among the pines, everything feels right.

So linger a moment, let time drift away,
Among frosted pines, let the spirit play.
In this winter's embrace, we find who we are,
Hidden among the pines, we shine like a star.

The Calm Between the Storms

In the hush, where whispers rest,
Clouds gather their heavy grace.
A moment caught, a fleeting guest,
Harmony enshrouds this space.

Branches sway with gentle ease,
Nature pauses, breath held tight.
Cool winds carry the scent of trees,
Illuminated by soft twilight.

Sunset paints the sky so bright,
Radiance lingers, while storms brew.
Clouds in lines, a dancing sight,
Granting a peace, serene and true.

In this calm, we find our way,
Hearts unite in silent prayer.
Beneath the brooding skies of gray,
Love's quiet thread is woven there.

So let us cherish every breath,
Where beauty dwells and time suspends.
In storms, we find the dance of death,
But in the calm, our spirit mends.

Pockets of Winter Stillness

Amidst the snow, the world lies wide,
A blanket soft, untouched and pure.
Silence reigns, with secrets tied,
In winter's hold, we find the cure.

Frost-kissed branches, a crystal glaze,
Each breath a whisper, cold and sweet.
Dreams of spring in frozen days,
Nature waiting, calm and discreet.

Pine trees stand like silent guards,
Starlit nights, a tranquil waltz.
Footsteps heard on snowy yards,
Each sound a soft and gentle pulse.

By the fire, we gather close,
Hearts entwined in warmth and light.
In these pockets, we do not boast,
With every pause, connected, right.

Winter's breath, a fleeting guest,
But in its arms, we find our peace.
In stillness, we are truly blessed,
As time within us finds release.

An Abode of Crystal Quiet

In a realm where silence sings,
Whispers dance on icy air.
A hidden place that winter brings,
Sheltered thoughts are free from care.

Crystal shards like stars above,
Glisten brightly in the night.
Wrapped in dreams of warmth and love,
This haven glows with soft, pale light.

Footfalls echo through the halls,
Each step a note, a fleeting sound.
Echoes fill these quiet walls,
Where solitude and peace abound.

Nature weaves its art so fine,
In each corner, stillness gleams.
In this abode, our hearts entwine,
Cradled gently in our dreams.

So let us linger in this space,
Where time itself begins to pause.
In crystal quiet, we embrace,
A world existing without flaws.

Beneath the Moon's Cold Glow

Underneath the silver light,
Whispers float like softest sighs.
The world unwinds, embraced by night,
While shadows dance and softly rise.

Stars align in velvet skies,
Each twinkle a forgotten tale.
In moonlight's grasp, our spirits fly,
Boundless dreams on cosmic sail.

Time stands still in this embrace,
A tender touch of night's sweet breath.
In silent beauty, we find grace,
Through moments steeped in gentle depth.

So let us wander, hand in hand,
Where the night sings its serenade.
In this realm, together we stand,
With hearts alight, unafraid.

Beneath the moon's cold, silken glow,
We uncover the magic found.
In every breath, love's tender flow,
In evening's hush, our souls are bound.

Hushed Footfalls on Snow

In the stillness of the night,
Soft whispers trace the ground,
Each step a gentle sigh,
In this quiet, peace is found.

Moonlight dances on the drifts,
Casting shadows, silver bright,
Footprints fading, like the mist,
Lost to dreams that take their flight.

Trees stand guard, their branches bare,
Adorned in blankets white and light,
Nature holds its breath in prayer,
In the embrace of winter's might.

The world beneath a canvas white,
Hushed together, time feels slow,
Every heartbeat feels so right,
In the trace of footfalls' glow.

As dawn awakens, colors play,
Golden rays through frosty air,
Hushed footfalls mark the way,
In this wonder, hearts lay bare.

The Sound of Shivering Shadows

Underneath the quiet sky,
Shadows dance in gentle flurries,
Velvet dark where secrets lie,
In their movements, silent stories.

Faint echoes of the night's embrace,
Whispered tales of lost desires,
In the chill, a fleeting grace,
Flickering like fading fires.

Moonbeams cast a silver sheen,
Over forms that twist and bend,
In the stillness, shadows glean,
The memories they long defend.

Thoughts drift softly on the breeze,
Carried on the breath of night,
Wrapped in whispers, minds find ease,
In the dark, there's hidden light.

With every shiver, stories shift,
The night a canvas for the brave,
In the sound of shadows' gift,
Awakens what the heart can save.

Beneath the Veil of Snowflakes

Gently falling, soft as dreams,
Snowflakes waltz on winter's breath,
Each one dances, fleeting gleam,
Whispers of a world in depth.

Beneath this veil, the earth is hushed,
Time stands still in crystal light,
Every moment feels so rushed,
Yet in this, everything feels right.

Footprints trace the stories told,
Each path a journey not forgot,
In glistening white, the world unfolds,
Where beauty lies, hidden, sought.

A silent hymn, the winter sings,
In snowflakes' soft, embracing fall,
Underneath, the heart still clings,
To the warmth that winter calls.

Embracing cold, we stand in awe,
Cradled in this joyous wrap,
Underneath the gentle paw,
Of snowflakes that lull the world to nap.

Chill in the Dusk

As daylight fades, the chill descends,
Whispers through the barren trees,
The evening sky, where twilight blends,
With shadows drawn by cooling breeze.

Each breath a fog, a moment's pause,
The world wrapped in a dusky hue,
Nature bows to winter's cause,
As colors fade to deepening blue.

Stars flicker softly, like old flames,
In the vault of growing night,
Each one holding long-lost names,
Guiding us with borrowed light.

The chill it speaks in hushed tones,
Through valleys deep and hills so steep,
In shadows cast, our silence moans,
As dusk unfolds, our thoughts will keep.

In this embrace, we find our way,
Through quiet moments, hearts entwined,
Chill in the dusk, where dreams will play,
A promise of the night redefined.

The Serenity of Icy Stillness

In winter's grasp, all is calm,
The world wrapped tight in a white balm.
Whispers of frost cloak each bare tree,
Nature's hush sings a soft decree.

Moonlight dances on frozen streams,
Casting shadows on forgotten dreams.
Crystals glisten, a starry delight,
In the heart of the tranquil night.

Silence reigns where the wild things roam,
Each flake's descent feels like a poem.
Beneath the chill, life takes a pause,
Reflecting on its hidden cause.

Footsteps crunch on the blanket white,
Echoes fade into gentle night.
Embraced by cold, the world feels right,
In this peaceful, wintry sight.

With each breath, the crisp air flows,
A fleeting moment, quietly glows.
In icy stillness, truth is found,
In the heart of winter's sound.

Dreaming in the Deep Freeze

In a world where frost blooms bright,
Dreams take flight in the quiet night.
Snowflakes whisper soft and low,
Carrying thoughts on the cold wind's blow.

Each breath hangs like a silver thread,
Painting visions in white and red.
Frozen lakes mirror the sky,
Reflecting wishes that never die.

Nature's canvas, stark and clean,
Hides secrets beneath layers unseen.
Creatures slumber, tucked in tight,
Safe from the chill of bitter night.

Underneath the thick, soft snow,
Memories linger of long ago.
In dreams we wander, free and bold,
Through the landscapes of winter's hold.

As dawn approaches, shadows creep,
Awakening stories from their sleep.
In the deep freeze, hearts ignite,
Breathing warmth into the icy light.

Secrets in the Snowdrift

Upon the hill where silence lies,
Snowdrifts hide both truths and lies.
Each mound a tale of whispers past,
Guarding memories that forever last.

Tracks of creatures softly tread,
Map the journeys of those who fled.
In every flake that falls from grace,
Lives a story, a hidden place.

Ghostly nights weave through the air,
Clandestine meetings; few are aware.
Beneath the blanket, warmth does grow,
As secrets buried softly show.

The crunch of snow beneath my feet,
Unveils the path where cold winds greet.
I trace the lines where shadows play,
In the snowy depths where dreams lay.

As daylight breaks, the world awakes,
The frost reveals what winter makes.
In these drifts, both light and shade,
Lies a tapestry nature made.

A Symphony of Shivers

The winter winds begin to howl,
In harmony with the moonlit prowl.
Frosted branches sway and bend,
Nature's music without end.

In each shiver, a note is played,
A song of ice and shadows laid.
Echoes dance through the crisp night air,
Weaving rhythms both wild and rare.

From silent peaks to valleys low,
The symphony of frost does grow.
Chirps of owls and whispers of snow,
Create a magic that ebbs and flows.

Shimmering stars twinkle above,
Casting down their winter love.
In the harmony of cold delight,
The world finds peace in the quiet night.

Amidst the chill, the heart finds cheer,
In this symphony, crystal clear.
A celebration of winters past,
In a world where echoes last.

Lullaby of the North

The whispers of the cold wind blow,
Gentle dreams in soft white snow.
Moonlight dances on frozen streams,
Nights are woven with silver dreams.

Crickets hush, the world lies still,
Stars above with twinkling thrill.
The pines stand tall, they guard the night,
Cradling secrets in soft moonlight.

A lullaby sung by the trees,
Soothing hearts with the northern breeze.
Echoes of stories, old and wise,
Floating gently beneath dark skies.

In the quiet, the heart finds peace,
Nature's song will never cease.
Beneath the blanket of starlit glow,
Dream sweet dreams, let worries go.

The night drapes softly over the land,
A tender touch by Mother's hand.
In the hush, let the spirit soar,
For in the north, you'll find much more.

Inward Reflections

In the mirror of the soul, we gaze,
Unearthing thoughts lost in a maze.
Each shadow dances, a fleeting glance,
Revealing truths in life's deep trance.

Silent whispers of heart's desire,
Fueling dreams like a quiet fire.
Moments flutter like moths at night,
Yearning for warmth, drawn to the light.

In stillness comes the mind's embrace,
A gentle touch, a sacred space.
Thoughts converge like streams on a quest,
Seeking solace, finding rest.

Reflection's journey, winding slow,
Understanding blooms where shadows grow.
Unraveling threads of joy and pain,
Connecting hearts like summer rain.

In each heartbeat, a story sung,
In every silence, a song begun.
The inward path leads us to see,
The beauty of simply being free.

Silence Wrapped in Snow

In the hush of winter's breath,
Snowflakes drift, a dance of death.
Covering all in a soft white shroud,
Whispering secrets, quiet and loud.

Trees wear coats of frosted lace,
Nature pauses, slowing the pace.
Footsteps muffled, all sounds fade,
In this silence, stillness is laid.

Frozen lakes reflect the stars,
Holding dreams, bound by winter's scars.
Each crystal glimmers, a silent vow,
To hold the world in a frozen bow.

With every breath, the air is clear,
A moment cherished, year after year.
Time stands still, wrapped tight in snow,
Listening softly to the world's gentle flow.

In this quiet, we all can find,
A peace that stills the restless mind.
Silence sings, a calm decree,
In the heart of winter, we are free.

Constellations above the Ice

Underneath a velvet sky,
Stars awaken, bright and spry.
They paint a canvas, bold and wide,
Guiding dreams on a cosmic ride.

Each twinkle tells a tale so old,
Of brave explorers, warriors bold.
Northern lights, a dazzling dance,
Nature's wonder, a timeless chance.

The ice reflects the glowing hue,
A mirror of the dreams in view.
Galaxies swirl like thoughts in flight,
Carving paths through the endless night.

With every star, a wish is made,
Adventures held in the starlight's shade.
The universe whispers, soft and sweet,
In every heartbeat, a world to meet.

So gaze above, let your spirit soar,
In the cosmos, there's always more.
For constellations paint the skies,
A tapestry of hope that never dies.

The Beauty of Iced Serenity

Crystal flakes descend with grace,
Transforming earth into a lace.
Each shimmer basks in moonlight's glow,
A tranquil whisper, soft and slow.

Silent woods in white attire,
Embers of dusk, a fading fire.
Nature's breath in chilling air,
The frozen world, a beauty rare.

Footprints trace an ancient tale,
Woven paths in winter's veil.
The gentle hush, the still of night,
In this calm, all feels right.

Stars above, a twinkling show,
In the serene, they ebb and flow.
Each moment held in frosty hands,
A dreamscape formed where silence stands.

Glistening dawn begins to break,
Through icy panes, warm shadows wake.
A symphony of breathless sighs,
In frozen beauty, the heart lies.

Timeless Winter Whispers

Snowflakes dance like whispered dreams,
Beneath the hush, the stillness gleams.
Every tree a silhouette,
In the chill, the heart's duet.

Echoes murmur through the pines,
Nature weaves its subtle lines.
Footfalls soft on powdered ground,
In this moment, peace is found.

Frost-kissed branches catch the light,
As day surrenders into night.
Stars awaken, twinkling bright,
A tapestry of pure delight.

On the air, a silent song,
Where time stands still, we all belong.
In each breath, a story told,
Wrapped in warmth against the cold.

Winter's embrace, serene and wise,
Invites us to reflect and rise.
With every flake, a promise keeps,
The beauty in the stillness sleeps.

Echoes of a Snowy Dawn

Morning light breaks through the haze,
Painting white in soft arrays.
Winter's breath, a gentle sigh,
As the world wakes with a cry.

Snowflakes flutter, pure and bright,
In the hush of early light.
Whispers linger on the breeze,
Secrets held beneath the trees.

Fields adorned in diamond dust,
Memories wrapped in frost and trust.
Each moment holds a fleeting grace,
In nature's white, a sacred space.

Birds take flight, wings spread wide,
In the calm, their joy can't hide.
A new day dawns, so crystal clear,
With echoes of winter drawing near.

Let the silence guide the way,
Through the beauty of the day.
In every flake, a wish takes flight,
Echoes dance in morning light.

In the Quiet of Frozen Dusk

As the sun dips low and deep,
The world settles, begins to sleep.
A blanket white, so soft and still,
Time pauses with a calming thrill.

Shadows stretch in twilight's glow,
Frosty air begins to flow.
In quiet corners, secrets weave,
The night whispers, and hearts believe.

Stars emerge in velvet skies,
Softly glimmering, brightening eyes.
Nature holds its breath so tight,
In this hush, all feels right.

Snow-capped hills, a silent choir,
Chilling winds hum soft and dire.
With every glance, the heart finds peace,
In winter's grasp, a sweet release.

In the stillness, dreams take flight,
In the quiet, darkness takes light.
A frozen dusk's sweet song will stay,
Carrying thoughts until the day.

Winter's Whisper

The snowflakes dance from sky to ground,
A silent hush, a soft surround.
Beneath the moon, the world aglow,
In winter's arms, all time is slow.

Branches bare, they bow and sway,
As frosty winds begin to play.
Whispers travel on the breeze,
Nature's voice, a gentle tease.

Footprints lie in purest white,
Each step a mark in silent night.
The stars above, they twinkle bright,
A canvas painted, pure delight.

In cozy nooks, the warm fires burn,
As icy trails twist and turn.
The world outside is crisp and clear,
Winter's charm, we hold so dear.

So let us wrap in wool and thread,
Embrace the chill, from toes to head.
For in this frost, we find our cheer,
In winter's whisper, we draw near.

Chilled Echoes

The frost it clings to windowpanes,
Nature sleeps, but still remains.
Echoes of laughter, now subdued,
In winter's grasp, a quiet mood.

Trees stand tall, with coats of white,
Transforming day into starlit night.
A distant sound, a bird's soft call,
In chilled echoes, we hear it all.

The paths we trek, so crisp and neat,
With every crunch beneath our feet.
An icy breath upon our skin,
As winter's tale begins to spin.

The hearth awaits with warmth to spare,
As we gather close without a care.
Stories shared by crackling fire,
Chilled echoes stir our hearts' desire.

So watch the snowflakes, pure and free,
As they swirl through the frosty breeze.
For in these moments, we unfold,
Chilled echoes, tales of old.

The Quiet of Snowflakes

Gently falling, soft and light,
Snowflakes weave a quilt of white.
Each one unique, a work of art,
They land like whispers, every part.

The world transformed in silence deep,
Where time stands still, we pause and keep.
In frozen air, our breaths we see,
The quiet speaks, so peacefully.

Amidst the pines, the shadows blend,
Where branches hold the snow, our friend.
A tranquil hush, a serene glow,
In winter's grip, the heartbeats slow.

There's magic found in each soft flake,
In frozen dance, a chance we take.
A gentle sigh, the world holds still,
In quiet moments, we find our thrill.

So let us walk where nature sleeps,
Through quiet paths, where silence creeps.
For in the stillness, we find grace,
The quiet of snowflakes, our embrace.

Shattered Stillness

A crack of ice, the echo flows,
Breaking silence, winter's prose.
In valleys low, the sound resounds,
A symphony where peace abounds.

The frozen lake, a mirror clear,
Reflecting dreams, both far and near.
With every jab of nature's knife,
Shattered stillness gives us life.

Footsteps crunch on paths once bare,
Each sound a note in winter's air.
The chilly breeze, it stirs the soul,
In shattered stillness, we find whole.

Birds take flight, on wings of grace,
Against the backdrop, they embrace.
The thrill of life, it intertwines,
With shattered stillness, nature shines.

So linger here where echoes play,
In the warmth of this frosty day.
For in the cracks, our spirits rise,
In shattered stillness, we find skies.

www.ingramcontent.com/pod-product-compliance
Ingram Content Group UK Ltd.
Pitfield, Milton Keynes, MK11 3LW, UK
UKHW031940151224
452382UK00006B/227